Naval Heritage in the

by Andy Endacott

PART I

1910
"I am leaving this evening, will write as soon as I can after getting to my destination — with love".

Cover Picture HMS ST. VINCENT was a vessel of 120 guns displacement 4672 tons and built at Devonport in 1814. Although ready to be launched on time she was left on the slipway and covered in to season as recommended by R. Pering, the Clerk of the Cheque (Cashier). This revolutionary method of preventing premature decay of the ships, gave rise between 1815 and 1820 to permanent covers over ships and docks in South Yard (see Pages 13, 25 and 46).

Quotation

"May the day be far distant, when the people of Great Britain, shall in the security of luxurious ease, forget the services of her right arm – the Navy – may it never be withered by the chilly breath of neglect. If our country be true to herself, that day never will be permitted to arrive, for it will be the last of England's greatness".

Quotation from 'The Stranger's Hand Book to the Western Metropolis', dated 1841.

ISBN 0 9511527 0 X
First published: August 1986

Published by D L ENDACOTT, 58 GLENHOLT ROAD, PLYMOUTH, and printed by Hitchings and Mason Ltd., West Hoe Road, Plymouth, Devon.

INTRODUCTION

Over the years I have felt that someone should put on record some of the pictorial history of the River Tamar and its industries. The idea became more alive after starting a collection of old postcard views and it seemed apparent that the Dockyard and the River Tamar area would be a good subject.

"All the nice girls love a sailor" and "a sailor has a girl in every port", or so the sayings go. But also, in many ports, a sailor had a more serious ally that he was attached to, a Dockyard with full maintenance and repair facilities.

Since 1689, when the Dockyard and surrounding area (known as Plymouth Dock) was established on the River Tamar, and from 1824, when it was renamed Devonport, the handling of the Navy's needs has been and, we hope, will be the prime industry of the whole area.

Back in 1625 when areas were being examined for siting the Dockyard, Saltash and its thriving port were considered and would have been chosen, except that the hardy fishermen of Saltash declared it would destroy their industry, thus robbing them of their livelihood and even their gardens and surrounding lands. So, Cornwall was that close to having the Dockyard on its soil. Still, the River Tamar and Hamoaze have given rise to many spin-off areas, in particular Torpoint, or 'Tar Point' as it was known, where the ships were beached and the hulls caulked and tarred.

Torpoint was created to be the accommodation site for the Dockyard families, and it still produces a substantial work force to this day. Further inshore, the Naval Seamen Training Establishments of *HMS Raleigh* and *Fisgard* have been the naval spin-off industry from the Dockyard.

The River Tamar has supported wooden walled ships of the line, iron clads, battleships, aircraft carriers, and now, in the Twentieth Century, the nuclear submarine.

The commercial and private hire users of the river are the daily passenger and transport carrying ferries between Devon and Cornwall, and the tourists on such river excursions as "Visit the Dockyard and Warships".

Last journeys of both *"Eagle"* and *"Ark Royal"* aircraft carriers commenced from their moorings at Cremyll, and recently the Port saw the return of the triumphant armada of ships back from the Falklands.

Equally important to the Navy is the Victualling area, i.e. Royal William Yard, to feed and clothe the fleet.

Also along the shore line in past years have been Ordnance Yards and Gunpowder Stores, and these areas have been upgraded to meet modern ship requirements.

The Dockyard has expanded from the Plymouth Dock era with a workforce of only 75 and only 24 acres in size (would fit within the present large Prince of Wales basin) to a World War One capacity of over 15,000 and now to a yard covering a water frontage of 2½ miles, with 14 Docks and 313 acres, and many Basins and Complexes for specialist work and a present workforce of over 12,000.

Regardless who controls the industry, the association of the River Tamar and its ships and support areas will hopefully be maintained to its usual high standards and traditions.

Meanwhile, the ferry links and the inland road and rail bridges will continue to serve between Devon and Cornwall for all.

Many of the photos used are part of a postcard collection of mine which I started about 5 years ago and, where applicable, I have used information from the *other* side to support an interest in the picture.

I would like to thank Syd Goodman for encouraging me to explore my own knowledge of the subject and for the additional help of photographs from his own collection. Thanks are also due to Jim Broad and the late Jack Kingston, both residents of Torpoint, who allowed me to tap a little of their wealth of information on the Tamar and loaned some fine prints, to Harold Ross for his contribution of photos and literature, and to Cliff Trethewey and Marshall Ware. It would seem that we have a common bond in preserving the history of this fine area. Finally, to the mainstay behind any publication task, a long-suffering wife, who has to see all, hear all and seem interested as well. In this case, Marilyn has done a tremendous job — correcting spelling and grammatical errors, typing, retyping and retyping again to the final manuscript.

My hope is that you, the reader, will be sufficiently impressed by these combined efforts to look around eagerly for the next instalment. It is anticipated to produce a follow-on edition to this volume showing updating of areas and equipment used on this famous West Country River and other places.

© D. L. ENDACOTT
58,Glenholt Road,
Plymouth PL6 7JD.

August 1986

"KING BILLY" in full regal splendour enjoys a commanding view over the waters of the Hamoaze which have borne the pride of the Royal Navy from Wooden Wallers to Nuclear Submarines.

EXTENT OF RIVER AREA COVERED

The Royal Albert Railway Bridge, built by Brunel in 1859, spanning between Devon and Cornwall, with the Saltash transport-carrying ferry leaving from St. Budeaux on the Devon side. The ferry is guided across between sets of chains, which can be seen on the slipway. It is situated at the top end of the River Tamar.

This is the lower end of the River Tamar just before it blends into Plymouth Sound, behind the Royal William Yard Buildings. The twin-funnelled paddle vessel was the C in C's yacht — *HMS VIVID* — and the building in the water was a covered bathing tray used by naval officers and guests.

ON THE RIVER SCENES

H.M.S. Impregnable, Flagship, Devonport.

HMS HOOD, one of the Royal Sovereign Class, circa 1892, can be seen mid river. The landing stage, called North Corner, was a floating pontoon connected to the land by a bridge structure and from there a journey to Millbrook in Cornwall could be made in a passenger steamer. This service was discontinued in 1964 after nearly 40 years. The roofed building has since gone, the sides of the Bridge have been steel plated and riveted, and the wooden frameworks have been replaced by vertical steel guides encased in concrete. Local fishing enthusiasts now enjoy the vantage point of the floating platform.

See opposite page.

The Victualling Office at Devil's Point, circa 1829. Here we can imagine the scene of crews taking on board such items as salt, the chief preservative, biscuits, cheese, butter, beef, pork, fish, peas and beer as their main foods, with sugar, oatmeal, cocoa and casks of fresh water.

With their Training Ship, *HMS Impregnable,* mid-channel, these young seamen are scraping, painting and cleaning their 12-oared cutter on Cremyll Beach, before returning to the parent ship. The paddle Steamer *"Britannia"* lies astern of the screw steamer *"Lady of the Lake"* just offshore.

NAVAL TRAINING ABOARD SHIP

Training Ship. Instruction by Model.

Below decks on the wooden walled floating School, these young seamen were constantly under the watchful eye of the ship's permanent staff during lessons.

Wash day about *HMS IMPREGNABLE,* the training ship moored off Cremyll Beach. Note also the numerous cutters in their davits, which would have been in constant use for exercises in seamanship.

Opposite Page Top

Learning the facts of any job from a text book has always been hard work. But here, with the aid of a third-dimensional workable model, the application of sail handling ropes and pulleys can be clearly understood, with less chance of an accident than in the actual situation.

KEYHAM YARD

HER MAJESTY'S NEW STEAM-YARD, AT KEYHAM.

Here we see the newly built area of the Yard in 1835. The view on the right is of No. 1 (South) Dock, No. 2 (Middle) Dock and No. 3 (Queen's) Dock containing *HMS QUEEN*. The building at the head of the Docks is the Machine Shop and behind to the left is the Police Station building and entrance to the Yard. Behind the stern of the ship in dock is the Carpenters' Shop and Shipwrights' Shed and to its rear is the Quadrangle Complex of buildings. A composite Sail/Steam vessel is moving across No. 2 Basin and many goose-neck cranes are sited around the various berthing positions.

Looking towards No. 2 South Basin from midway along No. 3 (Queen's Dock). The sheer legs can be seen sited on the basin edge, and the main building was the Carpenters' Shop and Shipwrights' No. 3 Shed. The chutes cut periodically along the stepped slopes of the Dock allowed staging planks and other materials to be lowered easily to the Dock Bottom.

This Torpedo Boat Destroyer (early 1900's) was an early development of the Destroyer, and is seen entering No. 2 (Middle) Dock (now No. 6 Dock). After the dock was built, modifications were carried out to recess the lower altars, to allow paddle wheeled vessels to enter with their wheels still in position. The long building was a Work Shed and Battery Shop, and at the far end of the dock was the Paint Shop. Part of the Quadrangle and MCD Joiners' Shop can also be seen. Note the heavy-lifting sheer legs sited around the berthing positions.

Destroyer entering Dock, Devonport Dockyard.

The *"QUEEN"* battleship of 116 guns in No. 3 Dock. On the opening day of the Keyham Steam Yard, 7th October, 1853, she moved into this dock with men manning the yards, and in commemoration this dock has since been referred to as Queen's Dock. In the background can be seen the outline of the Keyham Steam Pump House on the outer area of South Basin.

RIVER MOORINGS

HMS IMPLACABLE and *LION* moored mid stream with the Naval Barracks in the background. The young seamen went aloft to the mast and spars doing various drills. 'Implacable' served at Trafalgar and then became the first Royal Naval Training Ship in 1860 and remained at Devonport.

HMS IMPREGNABLE, another Naval Training Ship, moored opposite the southern end of the Dockyard and adjacent to Cremyll. The covered-in slipways at this, the widest, part of the river were ideally positioned for successful big ship launches.

RIVER FERRIES

This ferry, built by Hocking of Stonehouse Poole in 1835, was the second designed by J. M. Rendel. One of the river hulks at anchor was the *LEDA*, the Police accommodation ship for themselves and their families, to keep them away from bribery and corruption attempted by the Dockyard employees. The large building on the Gun Wharf contained the Workshops and Armoury Section.

The down river ferry *ALBERT* landing passengers at the Public Jetty at Saltash. She was the last steam ferry to work from Saltash and North Corner and finished in 1925. The Chain Ferry has landed and the horse drawn traffic is leaving the main central deck. Sheep and cattle were herded across on this deck, but thankfully the passengers sat on the top decks either side. When the coach and horses were being carried, the passengers had to remain in or on top of the Coach.

One of the many ferry boats which ran a service from Devonport to Saltash, shown approaching Saltash, with Dockyard maties at the end of a day's ship repair work.

MUD FLATS TO DRY DOCKS

Because of the angle of the shore line, it became easier to seal off the site and commence work on this first dock No. 8 to the new Complex area. At this early stage the head of the dock was squared across, but at a later period it was extended and tapered. Here the large granite stones of the inner sill for the Caisson are being fitted in.

See Opposite page.

Over 4 million cubic yards of mud was removed from this site and taken in barges, out past the Plymouth Breakwater and 4 miles beyond, before being dumped. The jetty from the shore was 1300ft. long and started at the lower end of the Barracks Parade Ground and went diagonally across (south-westerly) into the river moorings at the low tide positions. The Tamar Barge, called *WILLIAM & THOMAS,* is beached at the high water mark area (in the present area at the head of No. 8 Dock).

The double headed pile driver is being used to construct the timbered Coffer Dam across a position parallel and in front of the eventual entrances to Nos. 8, 9 and 10 Docks. *HMS GORGON,* Cyclops Class Monitor, is at anchor behind the pile driver near the end of the jetty. Laying in reserve is the white hulled Comus Class Cruiser. She was a sail/steam vessel with a steel hull which was sheathed in timber, and again copper clad, as a method of combatting sea growth, etc.

On February 21, 1907 the Prince of Wales, accompanied by the Princess, formally opened the NORTH DOCKYARD extension, proceeding into the Dock via the Lock, aboard the Admiralty yacht *"VIVID"*. The extension had taken over 10 years from the start to complete, using over 2,000,000 cu.ft. of granite from Cornwall and Norway and 220,000 tons of cement from the Thames, to convert 114 acres of marsh and low tide area into the largest Docks in the world.

See Opposite page

The North Lock with caisson openings at each end could be used as a Dry Dock, or the entrance for ships into the closed basin at various states of the tide. Because the site for the entire Complex had been cleared of vast amounts of mud and rock to give a level area, the floors of the Docks were built first, followed by the walls to the Lock and 10 Dock, and the remaining spaces between were then filled in. We are looking southward, with the east inner wall of the Lock being built up of granite blocks, cut according to size requirements at the Quarry works.

These souvenir postcards showed the magnitude of the Great Dockyard Extension, which was celebrated and recorded as a great building and engineering achievement at the beginning of the Century. The presence of the Royal Couple at the proceedings added to the celebrations. The initial idea of the New Basin was to moor the ships in reserve which were at that time in the Hamoaze (see pages 21 and 48). Towards the end of building the idea of actually fitting out ships was conceived, and additional piers and facilities were therefore added.

At the southern ends of No. 5 and 6 Docks (now 9 and 10) showing the slider caissons in position. This allowed a ship to enter from the Tidal basin, as each dock could be reduced in length to two smaller docks using a mid caisson position. These ends were later sealed in, and in particular No. 10 Dock was so lengthened, and at the time made wider for the *"Rodney"* in 1938.

More ships of the Reserve, at Bull Point, a little further down the river. Laying off in a single line permitted normal river traffic to continue. Barges, etc. travelled from Plymouth to Calstock, New Quay and Morwellham Quay, with quantities of limestone, and later returned with arsenic, granite and agricultural produce, thus making the river a very busy area.

SLIPWAY TO DRY DOCKS

HMS FROBISHER, a 'Cavendish' Class Cruiser entering the water at the bend of the river from No. 3 Slip (now No. 4). She had just been launched by the Countess Fortescue on March 20th 1920. The ship was originally designed as a coal/oil burner, but due to a prolonged stay of nearly 8 years in the Dockyard, she was eventually completed as an oil burner.

The 'Aetna' paddle tug, assisting the manoeuvering to the dry docks of the newly launched *HMS KING EDWARD VII* on the 23rd July 1903. The large ram bow can be clearly seen as she is lightly loaded in the water, with only the hull, decks and bulkheads completed. This class of battleship was the first to be fitted with a balanced rudder since 1870, and they were also fitted with three different calibres of main armament, which was greatly criticised at the time. She was sunk by a mine in 1916 on her way to Belfast for a refit.

The ram bow of this battleship can be clearly seen. Also shown are the Roman Numeral draught marks, which were repeated amidships and back aft around the stern, and indicated the depth the ship was floating in the water. The two hawse pipes on the starboard side housed sheet and bower anchors, with just a bower anchor portside. The two rows of sidelights gave natural light and ventilation to the crew inside the massive steel hull form.

Looking back at the old-fashioned staging, suspended on wire strops and ropes around the bow of a cruiser in dry dock. Spar staging and large distances between levels gave excuses for scrambling or dropping down single wires, which sometimes resulted in twisted limbs and splintered hands. Paint and oil also collected on the planks, which were not always secured properly.

SLIPWAY TO COAL HEAP

Built at Devonport and launched in 1877, *HMS Pelican* was a composite sloop, i.e. powered by sail or coal/steam. She spent many years on the Pacific and West Indies Station and, in 1919, after fittings had been removed, became a harbour hulk in Sydney, Nova Scotia. In 1953 she was towed out to sea and scuttled with full Naval honours. Here we see her moored off South Yard, alongside the Scrieve Board and Mould Loft buildings.

See Opposite page

HMS Hibernia on No. 3 Slip (now No. 4 Slip) adjacent to the Scrieve Board, waiting to be launched on June 17, 1905. She was the first ship to go into the New Dockyard Extension at Keyham and the basin was specially flooded to accept her. At 453ft. in Length and 78ft. Beam, with a final displacement of 15,360 tons, she was manned by a crew of over 770. The Scrieve Board has been built over the old No. 4 Slipway, and under part of the flooring can be seen the old slipway and the movements of the tide. The derrick spars consisted of steel tubular masts from many ships and, where the names were known, brass name plates were fixed accordingly.

This Apollo class cruiser, *HMS Retribution,* is shown off South Yard, where she would be able to take on Stores. The vessel was built in the early 1890's and finally disposed of in the 1910-1914 period. The Dockyard Chapel to the left on the skyline was lost, and the long Officers' Terrace (built 1692) was badly damaged during the second World War by bombing.

Dear Albert,
This is a photo of a large crane, they are building. The whole of it will travel up and down and be used for coaling ships which will come alongside the jetty.
We have plenty of Dreadnoughts at Devonport just now, and things are busy at the Yard. I expect the Centurion will be launched in August.
Remember me to all . . . . . Oscar.

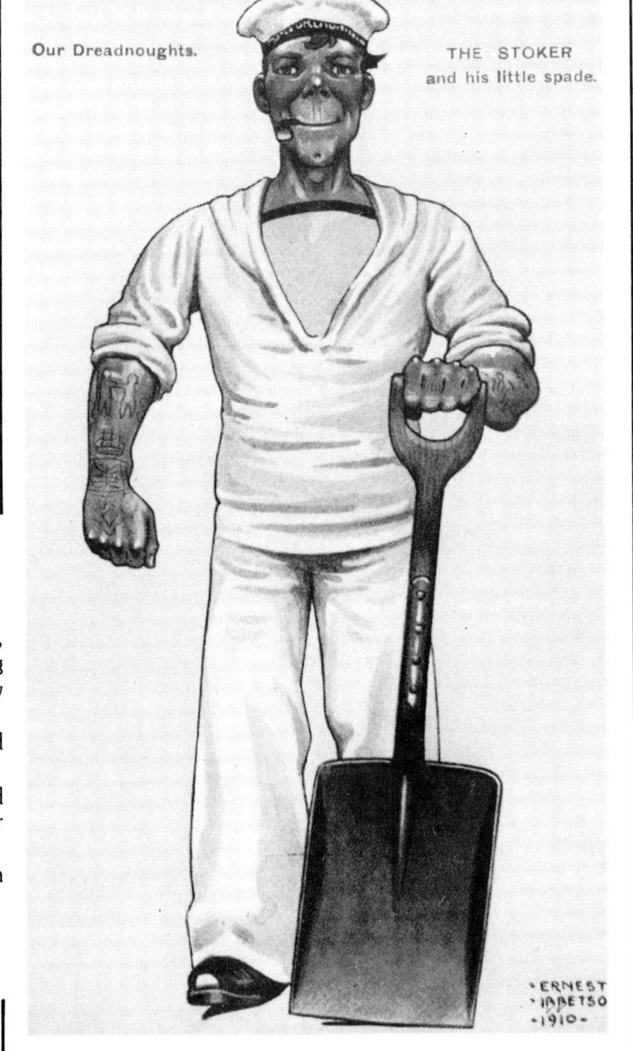

The Dreadnought's secret weapon the 'humble Stokes', always hard at work making steam. When it was the 'Coaling Ship' order, *everyone,* except the Captain and medically sick had to turn to and carry bags and buckets of coal.
Vaseline was supplied to push up the nostrils, and around the eyelids, and a headscarf and overalls were worn.
A meal of Corn Dog (corn beef sandwich), an apple, and Pusser's Kye (thick cocoa) was consumed on the upper deck areas.
Fire hoses were rigged, and the crew were sluiced down when emerging from below.

Moving to the other end of the Dockyard, we now see *HMS Centurion* tied up alongside the Coal Wharf, taking in her valuable fuel. She was built at Devonport in 1911, with a displacement of 23,000 tons, survived as a Radio Control Target ship and World War II Dummy Battleship and was finally sunk as part of the Mulberry Harbour system in 1944. Her captain, Joe Beckett (circa 1938) became Captain of the Dockyard and an authority on speeds of lorries. Whilst in his office in the Central Office Block, with the aid of a ship's sextant and stopwatch he could calculate the speed of passing vehicles and report them. For a long time drivers were unable to ascertain who was responsible and by what means they were being found out.
(Note: the speed limit at that time was 10 mph).

STONE WARSHIP LIFE

"Mess 23D, Block D, Royal Naval Barracks, Devonport.
Dear Auntie, You will see I have joined the Navy as a writer. There are about 7,500 sailors billetted here of different ranks, which is about double the peace-time numbers. We sleep in hammocks, which are about 6ft. off the floor, so you may guess the fun we have of getting into sleep. When I get settled I will write again . . . . . . Arthur".

These Blocks of Buildings were the first land accommodation areas for Naval personnel who had been paid off from their boats, and were built in the late 1880's, the Clock Tower being added in 1896. Previously, the men had been accommodated on old ship hulks in the river, awaiting another posting. In this view, about 1900, the area had been screened off in preparation for building the Wardroom Complex.

Keeping fit for active service, whether ashore or afloat, has been the responsibility of the P.T. Instructor. Wearing No. 5 canvas white trousers and seaman's jerseys, these ratings in the Gymnasium of Devonport Barracks, are being put through their paces.

When the Navy were called to go ashore to show the Flag, sometimes in action they would engage the enemy who was on horseback. This particular drill of a land engagement was necessary, even if not often used by the sailor. All drill to a young recruit seems unnecessary at the time, but during his career might be needed.

Field Gun Drill. R.N. Barracks, Devonport.

Big Gun Drill. R.N. Barracks, Devonport.

The not-so-friendly Bosun, exercising his vocal chords, endeavouring to convince the young seamen concerned that his way of doing things will be the best for everyone.

See opposite page

Action ashore training has now moved up in calibre. The speed of carrying these guns in pieces, transferring to horses and eventually assembling at the engagement of the battle, needed constant practice. Mount Edgcumbe Park and Obelisk Hill at Cremyll was a Naval training area for assembling and siting the gun on the supposed enemy in the river, having brought it ashore and climbed the hill first.
(See page 32).

A gun simulator was constructed for use in training the crew in loading procedures. Many of these gunnery tasks were later taken over by the Sea Soldiers, i.e. the Royal Marines. Note the rating rolling the large shell across the deck. Should the instructor find the trainee not paying attention he was made to carry in his arms a large shell on to the parade ground and then continue to hold the shell whilst shouting Naval commands and expressions at the top of his voice, until the punishment was deemed sufficient by the instructor.

GUNNERY SCHOOL

Young seamen going through the Gun Drill procedure, on the hillside overlooking the training ships near Cremyll.

In 1904, this Boer Gun was erected in memory of shipmates who had lost their lives in the South African War.
The grass turfs are just being laid by the workman, under the watchful eyes of the naval ratings.

HMS CAMBRIDGE and her tender *HMS CALCUTTA* were the two wooden walled vessels that formed the Devonport Gunnery School, on the River Tamar. HMS Calcutta was brought into the Keyham basin by a twin funnelled steam paddle box tug on October 29, 1907, followed the next day by HMS Cambridge, similarly assisted. A few days later, on November 4, came the final paying off of this familiar river floating school.

More seamanship instructions whilst below decks on the wooden waller. This time the lesson on steerage, with the aid of a model simulator platform.

NAVY AT WORK

In 1880, this College was opened purely as living quarters for the Naval students, whilst their practical on the job experiences were dealt with in the Dockyard. Over the years it has been extended, and Laboratories, classrooms, etc. have been built within. The Royal Naval Engineering College, as it was known, has seen many famous officers pass through its main entrance.

During the mid 1800's, Engineer Students did a 5-year apprenticeship. It was whilst completing the 5th year of training in the Dockyard that time was spent at the Smithy's Forge under the watchful eye of a dockyard Foreman. The working hours were very long — 6 a.m. to 6 p.m. daily, plus 2 compulsory evenings at Dockyard School until 8 p.m. and Saturdays until 3.40 p.m.

The young engineer did his first and fifth year in the Dockyard, which included a period of time in the Drawing Office, and three years at sea. In this shop the effort of filing machine block surfaces constantly eventually established the tolerances an engineer could work to, both by hand and by available machinery, when at sea doing maintenance and repairs.

The erecting shop was the area for assembling and repairing various types of engines. This section was but a small part of the Engineering Department called the Quadrangle, which covered about six acres. This vast complex housed such areas as the Boiler Shop, Plater's Shop, Foundry, Pattern Shop, Copper and Blacksmith's Shop and Fitting Shop.

4663 The Carpenters of a Battleship.

137 Make and Mend Day in H.M.S. Hindustan.

Whilst away at sea for long spells, many jobs have to be tackled by the crew. Here we see ropework and the blacksmith's ability to dress a ring bar around the anvil — just two examples of the early 'handyman'.

See opposite page.

All repairs to furniture and ships' boats and damage control work was carried out by the carpenters. As more steel was introduced, carpentry became limited to the Wardroom area and picture framing, etc. This petty officer watching the seaman at work is holding an adze — a tool for trimming spars and wood decks — in his right hand.

Life at sea, away from the comforts of home for as long as a couple of years, soon inspired the crew to attempt and master sewing and repair of their clothing. Many men developed artistic talents such as embroidery and clothes-making to occupy the long hours spent at sea. Many hobbies were developed, using all manner of materials, to fight the common enemy — "boredom at sea".

DOCKYARD ENTRANCES

This is the Fore Street Gate entance to the Southern end of the Dockyard. The large building inside was the Dockyard Chapel, rebuilt in 1817 after a previous fire, and finally bombed to an empty shell in 1941. Capable of seating 2,000 people, in strict seniority of rank, from the nave to the rear — the area for ordinary families.

This magnificent property was built in 1692 as Officers' Houses (13 in number) and became known as "The Terrace", commanding a grand view of the Yard. The Dockyard workmen are returning from their dinner break and are going down the cobbled slope to the many docks and workshops in South Yard.

Sparrow Park was to the left of the Albert Road Gates, alongside the entrance to the Dockyard Horse Drawn Fire Engine House. The Salvation Army would often stop and play many a fine tune beside the Park. Horse drawn cabs would also wait for fares from the Dockyard on the cobblestone space between the Park and the Gates.

Inside Albert Gate, with the original clock tower on the right, and the main archway entrance. Also on the right foreground is the rear of the Machine Shop. The building on the left was — and still is — the Police Station.

These men returning to their work would disperse all over the ship, to the places where their tool boxes were stowed, then change into overalls and go about their allotted tasks. The comparatively flimsy long brows have gradually been replaced over the years with a more rigid platform design, and solid hand rails to prevent men falling off. Tea-making was carried out on the dockside using either steam from the Naval Donkey Boiler, or a Dockyard wood-burning boiler. Using a metal tea can, tea and adding the hot water, the rich brew would be quickly carried up the Brow to the various tool box areas to be consumed.

OTHER ESTABLISHMENTS

The *"Mount Edgcumbe"* Industrial Training Ship was moored off Saltash from 1877 till 1920. Originally called *"Winchester"* and then *"Conway"*, she was used as a ship for homeless and destitute boys. Tuition in reading, writing, English Grammar and Mathematics, along with numerous nautical activities, was given to over 200 boys, some of whom eventually entered the Royal Navy. Here the photographer endeavoured to frame his ship subject between the granite pillar supports of Brunel Bridge, and also captured the attention of children bathing on the foreshore.

The *'Mount Edgcumbe'* training ship Band, which among other duties aboard ship, managed to give concerts on the St. Budeaux Green and at Church Bazaars.

MESSAGES & SIGNALS

The Naval Signal station on the high ground is seen with its mast and yards, displaying a single Ball. At 12 o'clock daily it was lowered in conjunction with a signal received from Greenwich and thus all the ships in the area would see this and their chronometers would be checked and adjusted.

When a ship was entering harbour, the order 'Attention on the upper deck, Face to starboard' was given when passing below Admiralty House at Mount Wise. Saluting the Admiral's Flag was a mark of respect, and at the same time the crew were aware that a telescope was looking over the vessel to see that everything was up to standard. This tradition is still carried out today.

The scanning eye of the Petty Officer looking for Signals, messages, and checking the dressage of a vessel.

RIVER TRAFFIC

The overcrowded cottages housed the watermen, whose business was to unload goods from the ships in the Sound. Naturally, smuggling played a part in some of the activities. The watermen also transferred daily passengers from the local Millbrook ferries on to the steps of the stone jetty. The perimeter wall of the southern end of the Dockyard can be seen behind the houses.

See opposite page

The Millbrook Ferry terminus at Devonport's Mutton Cove. Here we see the *"Lady of the Lake'* embarking passengers, via the Waterman's boat at the steps. In the background is the Naval Victualling Yard, and another boat returning to Millbrook with passengers.

The Cremyll-built boat *"Armadillo"* shown arriving at Admiral's Hard, Stonehouse. A horsedrawn cart is waiting, possibly to be taken with its provisions via a horseboat secured to the side of the steamer back to Cremyll. In the background are the railway carriages on Ocean Quay, on which passengers and produce from abroad were taken to London by the L.S.W.R. (circa 1912).

Here we see two designs of ferries at the Torpoint foreshore. The left hand vessel is the Summer ferry, built in 1878, and the other the Winter ferry, built in 1871. In the background is the *'Leda'* accommodation hulk, which was first moored alongside the Gun Wharf of the Dockyard in 1864, and finally sold for scrap in 1906.

At the mid river position is *HMS DEVASTATION* which was the vessel protecting the entrance to the Hamoaze. The river steamer *DEVONIA* is meanwhile sailing across to Mutton Cove from the Millbrook area. The large ship's hulk, which is *HMS CIRCE* was built in 1827, at one time a fifth rate of 46 guns. She became the tender to *HMS Impregnable,* and the Dockyard fitted her out as a swimming bath for boys under training in 1885. The rectangular vessel was also a Bathing Tray for the experienced swimmer. On the skyline are the covered-in slipways and Docks of South Yard.

NAVAL WELFARE

Miss Weston shaking hands with the Temperance Committee and presenting medals to the members of the Royal Naval Barracks, Devonport. Aggie founded the first Royal Sailors' Rest at Devonport in 1876, with the help of a friend. She did more in 50 years for the welfare of the Royal Navy than the whole Board of Admiralty. Miss Weston died in 1918 and was buried with full naval honours, the first woman to be given such a distinction. Over 2,000 officers and men were in attendance, and the roads from the Dockyard Chapel to the Cemetery at Weston Mill were lined with thousands of people waiting to say their last goodbyes. The coffin, covered by the Union Jack, was placed on a gun carriage.

Reserve Fleet of the Navy laying off moorings down river of the Saltash crossing. The *Mount Edgcumbe* training ship (see page 41) can be seen moored upstream of the bridge, behind the middle support.

Having finished his commission, and his ship having gone into reserve, or repair, the A.B. had two choices — either to go on leave to his family, taking gifts from abroad, or return to HMS Drake — Royal Naval Barracks, the stone warship (see back cover), and await a new posting.